Talking Tulips
(From Above and Below)

Written by Susan Billings Mitchell
Illustrated by Iwan Darmawan

Talking Tulips

Text and Illustrations Copyright © 2022 Susan B. Mitchell

Library of Congress-in-Publication Data
ISBN: 978-1-7335632-3-9 (hardcover)

Based on a true story as told by
Airman Evan A. Billings
of the US Army Air Corp.

Mette watched her father take down the red, white, and blue flag that hung on her family home for as long as she could remember. Mother was crying.

"We must be strong," her father said. Still he could not bring himself to hang up the "new flag." His country was neutral. Holland wanted no part of the war. Then why were they losing their precious FREEDOMS?

Evan hung a red-white-and blue flag over the
family porch and saluted it. His mother was
crying. Her son was barely old enough for the
Army Air Corp uniform he wore.

"Be strong" his father said.

One last time the young soldier looked into the
eyes of his would be sweetheart and then he
was off. His country needed him to help save
their precious FREEDOMS.

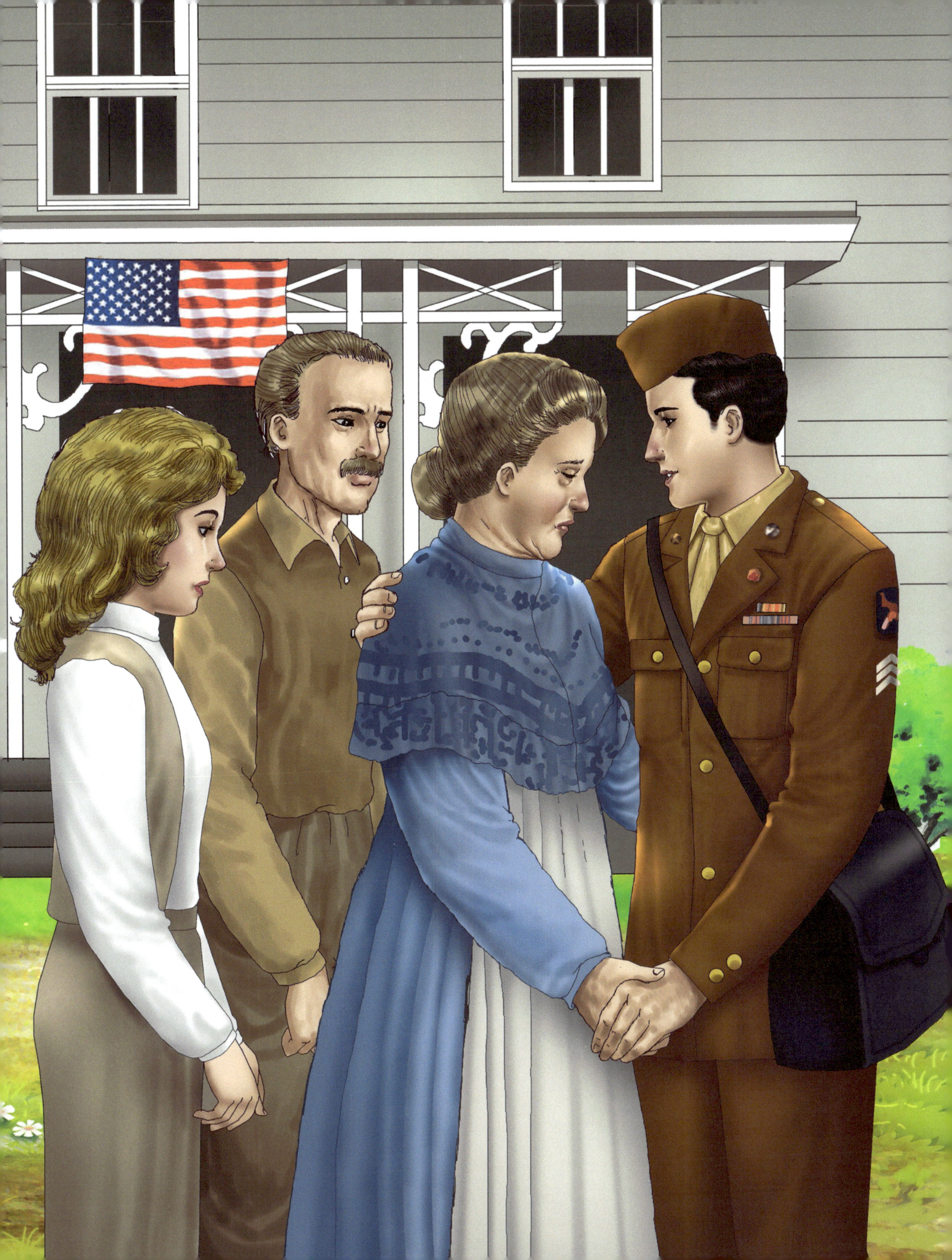

Nazi soldiers marched into Mette's classroom and pulled down the flag even when the school master told them not to touch it. They laughed at him.

"You belong to us now!" they said as they hung up a new flag.

Mette's heart filled with fear.

Allied soldiers rallied for the cause of freedom. They came from many lands, speaking many languages. Together they had to stop the Nazi Army in its quest to control the world.

Evan took courage in the fact that they were united in their hearts.

Below smoky skies, Mette looked out of the cottage window with a frown on her seven-year-old face. She could see father working in the tulip field and wanted to be with him. He used to take her along everywhere he went, but not anymore.

"Too dangerous," he told her. "There is a terrible war going on and we are caught in the thick of it!"

Above smoky clouds, Evan looked out of
his B-17 Bomber. Other planes flew so close
that their wings almost overlapped in tight
formation to prevent enemy planes from
separating them.

World War II had wrapped itself around
the earth like a dark, scratchy blanket. Evan,
a nineteen-year-old airman, sat right in the
middle of it.

Mette was hungry, so hungry her tummy hurt.
There was no food in the house; no food in
stores; no food in all of the Netherlands.

Nazi soldiers had blown up dikes and flooded
farmlands. They closed every road. No one
could leave. Nothing could enter.

Mette didn't like war. She didn't like bombs that
hurt people and broke things. She didn't like the
tulip bulbs mother boiled to eat. She was hungry,
so very hungry.

Evan was tired of Army K-rations that always left him hungry. On certain days, before each bombing mission, he and his crew were given a steak and potato dinner.

Around the table they talked about their Allied Forces surrounding the Nazi soldiers.

"Our men are holding them in place," someone said.

"The Netherlands is blocked by land and by sea. We'll starve those Nazis out," someone else said.

"What are the innocent people doing for food?" Evan wondered.

Mette cringed every time warplanes flew over her tulip fields.

"You must stay alert," her father said. "When you hear a siren, run for shelter."

Mette watched the street for enemy soldiers and listened for their marching feet. She didn't like to see the guns they carried or the spider-like symbol on their uniforms and flags. She wanted them to go away. Why did they keep coming, day after day?

Evan cringed every time he heard the order, "Bombs away." He watched the sky for enemy fighter jets.

"Stay alert," the pilot said. "They're coming in from behind."

Evan swung around and aimed the big guns. He didn't like to use them. Oh how he wanted to go home.

Day after day he climbed back into the top turret for a noisy ride across the sky.

Mette lay in darkness, unable to sleep.

Mother kissed her forehead and gently positioned her golden braids. "Think of happy times," she suggested.

Mette closed her eyes to picture Grandma's house, her flower gardens and her smiling face. How she longed to visit and put on an apron so she could help bake cookies.

Will I ever see Grandmother again? she wondered.

Evan lay restless on his cot, only hours away from the next bomb run. He closed his eyes to picture happier times with his family in their cozy farmhouse.

How he longed to taste his mother's apple pie, to pet Tippy his faithful dog, and to kiss Miss Mae, the girl he planned to marry.

Will I ever see her again? he wondered.

Bomber planes were loud and frightening to
hear. They seemed to pass over at any time
night or day.

Mette tried to be brave, even though the sound
of them turned her empty stomach.

Sometimes she sang songs to the baby and tried
to make him laugh about all the noise.

Bomber planes would shake and rattle as they
roared through the sky.

Evan tried to be brave even when he could see
through the holes left from flak explosions.

Often he tried to joke with other crewmen who
were also trying to be courageous.

K

The Netherlands was filled with starving people. Lack of nourishment made Mette so frail and weak she could no longer run for shelter when she heard planes coming, yet she sensed something was different. Never had they flown this low before, low enough to buzz the windmills. When she looked up, she thought she saw airmen waving to her. These planes didn't have the spider symbol on them!

"Mette, Mette," her father called. "Come and see."

His voice was happy. People laughed and hugged each other.

"Look at these bombs Mette. They are food bombs from our allied friends!"

With food in her tummy at last, Mette hurried
to help. Slipping into wooden work shoes she
started for the muddy tulip fields.

The dark night filled with happy, singing voices
of neighbors and kinfolk working side by side.
No one went to bed. Mette hauled away bucket-
loads of red tulip tops.

With a full heart Evan slept well for the first
time in months.

Early the next morning, he loaded more boxes
of K-rations into the bomb bay for another
food drop.

Evan listened to the talk in his headphones.
His crew hoped that the good people trapped
below had found the food bombs. If only there
was a way to be sure.

Suddenly loud cheering jerked the plane.
Yesterday's mission had been a success. How
did he know? Mette's tulips told him, loud and
clear in a way he would never forget!

THANKS

YANKS

ABOUT THE AUTHOR

War grabbed my father the day he graduated from high school. At such a tender age, He saw things no one should ever see and later refused to talk of them. I am not sure if his plane actually dropped the "food bombs" over The Hague (the seat of government in the Netherlands, and the capital city of the province of South Holland), but his description was so vivid I pictured him there. At any rate, I know it really happened.

How I wish I could acknowledge here all the names of the airman who took part. Also impressive to me is the fact that a gentle people who were neutral to the war effort were nonetheless imprisoned in their home-land and forced to live through destruction, loss, and starvation.

The purpose of this book is to show that BAD things happen to GOOD people, yet many choose to be kind, grateful, and full of light, even during dark times that befall them.